For Rachel and Zoe,

Thank you for always being by my side.

An Introductory Rambling…

The saying goes '*a problem shared is a problem halved*'.

I've always enjoyed writing. Writing stories on scraps of paper as a kid. Coming up with song lyrics during Lockdown. Scribbling my thoughts and feelings in journals.

In the summer of 2018, I was majorly triggered by my nan having a health scare and was desperate for a release. A friend of mine suggested writing about it so I opened up an old black A4 notepad and wrote it all out, and it's a process I haven't stopped since.

I've also been in and out of therapy with a range of counsellors over the past five years. I've dabbled in CBT, EMDR and talking therapies. Basically doing whatever I can to give myself the feeling of having my shit together. Spoiler alert: that feeling has never come.

During one particular session of EMDR, my counsellor at the time asked me to imagine myself strolling through a park and sitting on a bench. Then, she asked me to imagine a younger version of myself and talk to him. I embraced this younger-me, feeling a sense of sadness for all of the things that he's going to have to go through. In that imaginary place, I felt very protective of that younger version of myself. When I came back into the room, the counsellor made an effort to emphasise how, even through everything that has happened to me, I am still here.

I've spent five years sitting in many different counsellors' chairs. I have unpicked my childhood. I have discussed my journey towards accepting my sexuality. I have talked about my dating life and how I'm better off without them all. I've worked on embracing my abilities as a teacher. Even though I am still a work in progress, I can feel the progress that I've made on my journey.

In early 2024, I started going along to writing groups where we'd follow themed prompts and I found myself writing creatively about some of the things I've lived through. At first, I felt self-conscious to be sharing my personal experiences so openly with a table of strangers but over the six months I started to grow more confident in my writing style and letting these people in. Towards the end of the year, the lady who runs the groups announced that she is bringing her workshops to an end. This left me with my notebook full of anecdotes and poems, wondering what to do with them all now.

I turned up to a writer's social in town with my notebook, with two pages earmarked that I was keen to share as I just felt particularly proud of what I had written. I nervously read *Grievance* aloud, unsure of the response I'd get. "You should send it in to teaching magazines!" they suggested. Although I never heard back from any publications, I felt like maybe my writing was worth sharing for the first time.

For some reason, I signed myself up to a story-writing workshop and had a similar experience of other people saying they'd like to read my writing. They started discussing publishing and I began to look at my notebook differently. *What if I published this?* It wouldn't be from a place of craving success or wanting attention. I felt the process of collating everything I've written and releasing it into the world might give me some validation for my side of the story, and acknowledge that 2024 became one of those years that pushed me to my limit.

As 2024 came to a close, I'd finished my sessions with my third counsellor of the year and I felt ready to bring a lot of these chapters in my life to an end. What better way to do that than literally collating everything and then setting it aside?

One random evening, I created a folder in my Notes app, named it *Boyfriend Therapy* and I started typing out entries about the men I've dated. The process was therapeutic. Going through my notebook of writing, I felt like I was missing a thread to tie everything together and wondered if *Boyfriend Therapy* contained the pieces I was looking for. Between my anecdotes and poems, my *Boyfriend Therapy* entries provided the context to create a timeline of the past six years of my life.

I chose to start the timeline at my first boyfriend and how that intertwined with a friendship break-up in my early 20s, which is where I would pinpoint feeling like I didn't have my shit together for the first time.

As you read through my writing, I hope that some of it resonates with you. Maybe you've been in a similar position at work or met an interesting character like I have along the way. Counsellors always seem to ask me where I think my anxieties, self-doubts or 'other relevant issues' stem from. Hopefully by sharing this collection of pieces of writing with you, some of my problems may halve. Without further ado, here's the past six years of my life…

Ryan

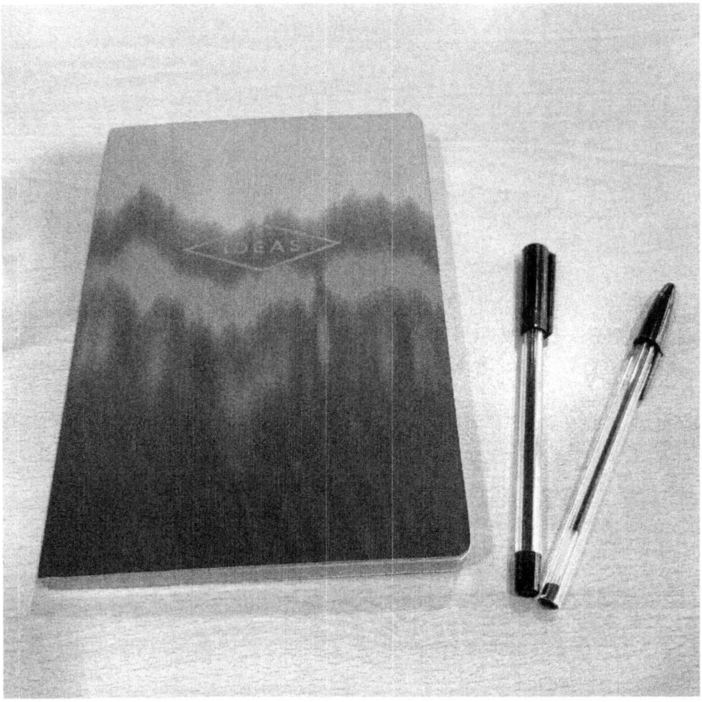
IDEAS

Closing a Chapter

Reflections and Revelations

by

Ryan Young

I HATE ENDINGS

No one talks about friendship break-ups. All of the self-help books, the Ted talks, the Instagram wisdom posts - they all relate to your partners. To me, my friends are *those* partners. How do you deal with that fracture?

My friends are where I've placed most of my commitments. Often, my friendships have outlasted my romantic relationships. The love is equally there for me, so isn't that the romance we strive for anyway?

One thought that circulates my brain is how every best friend I've had has left.

When a relationship ends, there's often a definitive closing. 'The break-up conversation'. A fine line drawn, dictating that you're no longer together.

When my friendships have ended, it's been much more gradual. Like sand falling through my fingers. Like ice melting past its freezing point.

The pain is as equally gradual. The question of what did I do? These have been the people that I've shared everything with, so who do I go to now?

The saddest part is once you've grown apart from enough of them, you just presume every friendship becomes finite, so you become wary of the ones who do want to be there.

I'm beginning to understand that the way to let that thought go is the affirmation that people come in and out of your life for a reason. If they were meant to stay, they would have.

Through all of these dating stories and different workplaces, my friendships are what have gotten me through it all, so this is for the ones who chose to stick around…

2018

A Beginning

Where It All Started.

My first boyfriend.
My reason for coming out.
After our first date, I didn't want to lie to my parents anymore about where I was going, so I chose to tell them that I was gay.
We were there for each other through university, our social circles intertwining, albeit not evenly as he had no interest in my friends.
We just seemed to click.
To those around us, we were the goal, two best friends who had a relationship together.
On the inside, we were a candle that burnt itself out.
We were young and three years was a very long time.
It worked at the time, but didn't survive once we left our university bubble.
We'd survived my inability to learn what my alcohol tolerance was.
We'd lasted despite his incessant reminders that "it's not like we'll stay together forever".
We'd worked through each other's issues with our friends.
We'd gotten over him still having dating apps after a year together with the reason being "window-shopping".
In the end, distance drove us apart, especially once I started working and he was struggling to find a job.
In hindsight, our relationship was dead in the water by the time I actually broke up with him, the catalyst being my drunken urge to kiss someone else.

As much as I regretted it, and part of me still does now, I knew deep down it happened because my relationship was no longer making me feel good about myself and I didn't know any better.

The closure came for me several months later, when we met up again. Whilst I was hoping we could have another try, he made it very clear that he was over me. The crushing line spoken was 'I still fancy you, but I don't love you anymore'. I cried. He hugged me but his embrace felt like a stranger's. The words weren't what upset me. It was the realisation that we'd never be able to get back what we had. Once I composed myself, I said "there's nothing here for me anymore" and headed home.

Rachel collected me from the train station that day and drove me to the beach, with Olly Murs blasting out of the stereo, to throw stones into the sea in the darkness. I am forever grateful for what she did that evening as it reminded me of the love that I still had in my life, even without his, and she's supported me through every man since.

There Will Be Blood

We travelled to Lokrum Island via her Aunt and Uncle's boat. We were pre-warned of how Aunty is very blunt. This disclaimer was clearly warranted when she'd turned to him and said "oh, you've gained much kilo since photo…". Clearly her broken English will break him.

The sea there was beautiful. Peaceful. The deep blue you see in brochures. No one around. Peacocks strolling by. It came to our lunchtime and the opening of our packed sandwiches. Somehow, the ants found his, I've never seen him *this* pissed off. It's not like I could share either as mine was ham…

Then came family-style dining, the Croatian way. Platters of seafood and meat were placed in front of us all. Squid, baby fish, sausages. You name it, it was there. Then the Uncle's face screwed up. Even in his curt Croatian mumbles to his wife, I figured it was a reference to why the vegetarians weren't eating. *Uh oh, he's not impressed.* I guess it's on me to sample what Croatia has to offer us…

As for him, I can't say this will be his favourite day of our trip…

Teleportation

The sunset seemed to hit differently there.

Yellows, oranges, pinks.

All a backdrop to surround the palm trees.

Carrying tote bags of Fantas and Cokes.

Walking across the cooling sand.

Finding a nice spot for the four of us.

A faraway island in the distance - one we'll visit tomorrow.

Tonight, we're watching the sun go down.

Stripping down, clothes in a bundle, treading the water.

My first time in the sea.

That feeling of not feeling the bottom.

There's a warmth that you don't feel at home.

This Is Just To Say…

Forgive me

        for laughing

        when cooking

        with you.

Red velvet cracked,

        sponge split,

        nothing left

        for us to do.

You were furious

        at yourself, at me.

        We're now the same.

        Hopeless bakery.

Growing Together, Growing Apart

"Fuck our Toms!" shouted in unison.

Nicki Minaj's bum-inspired birthday cakes.

Taylor Swift's *1989* polaroids pinned on the wall.

Tumblr gifs reblogged to and fro.

Belting out *New Rules* in questionable matching cat costumes.

Kissing people we shouldn't be.

Side-eyes lurking in backgrounds.

Envy emerging at the other's success.

Instability screaming between the lines.

Dependency pushing us apart.

"I've had nothing to say," she says.

A week becomes two.

A month becomes a few.

Grew together, grew apart.

Still asking myself "what did I do?".

The One I Let Go Of

Hindsight made me realise I let a good one go here. He was a bit older than me and was the first guy I'd dated after breaking up with my first boyfriend. I was not ready to move on but I didn't know that yet, so I spent the whole summer getting to know this guy by comparing him to what I'd had. He seemed closed off at times, which I think was down to our age gap and him being and in a more stable position. We talked about our lives but never about how we felt towards each other. After a few months, my Nan found some cancerous tissue and I panicked, which led me to start journalling as an outlet. I felt like I couldn't tell him about what was happening for some reason. I didn't feel like I was ready to lean on him yet and that was the evidence I needed to justify that he wasn't the one for me.

Woodberry Avenue

I press the doorbell nervously.
It's been six months since I've been here.
I stare through the cracked, stained glass,
Awaiting some sign of movement,
And then it's opened.
He's there, smiling back at me,
But something feels off immediately.
The atmosphere feels awkward,
The familiarity has gone.
Although the hallway is as it was,
I'm searching for anything to bring back what we had.
The mirror that we'd taken selfies in together.
The banister that he'd always complain about if I hung up my coat.
The wooden doors leading to rooms only used for entertaining.
However, this feels like a place where I'm no longer welcome.
No longer am I a part of this.
I'm now an intruder.
"You've got branded shoes now?" He quips,
Noticing how I've branched into Vans over the summer.
"You're in pink?" I reply,
Acknowledging the colour I've never seen him in.
He stood on the stairs, looking down at me.
That was when I felt that everything had changed.

Texture

Oh fuck… texture.

Every time, it comes to this moment.

Sharing my admission with the next person,

That I am a fussy eater.

I'm not really sure when it became embarrassing,

But I feel a sense of shame every time I have to craft a response,

Usually to the follow-up question of "so what *do* you eat?"

My brain scrambles through the examples of beige dinners,

In the hope of something vaguely adventurous,

Often accompanied by a nervous laugh,

Feeling the need to explain that my idea of hell…

… is a five a day.

A Naive Excitement for Dessert

Bowls being passed along the table excitedly.

Sure, why not, I'll have one.

This looks different.

A sweet, warm-smelling, crumbly texture.

Thick custard sliding off the golden surface.

Steam rising above.

A sugary smell luring me in to my first bite.

Hmmm…

This tastes unusual.

A twang I'm not used to.

Part toffee, part something else.

I can't put my finger on it.

I have another bite, swallowing curiously.

Then someone blurts out…

"You can really taste the banana in this!"

Oh no…

Gilet Man

This was one of those situations where I found myself walking up to the restaurant we'd agreed to meet at, seeing a man waiting outside wearing a gilet and thinking 'oh no'….

We walked in, sat at our table and our evening began. He said he was studying rural agriculture. That was what his passion was and drive is always interesting in a person.

What I didn't realise was that his *real* passion was politics. "Are you into politics?" "No," I replied, probably too bluntly, as I was much more interested in what the Kardashians were up to than whatever Theresa May was doing. Well, little did I know that I was sitting across from a local Conservative representative for the area. "Would you like to see my leaflets?" he asked, showing me a photo of a load of leaflets he'd printed. I asked him if he goes knocking from door to door. *Yes, yes he does*. I also gathered that he had rescheduled our date because he had gone to the Conservative Party Conference. The one where Theresa May had walked on stage to Dancing Queen.

Out of the blue, he bluntly goes "shall we get the bill because my car parking is almost up?". So we split the bill, say goodbye and that's that. Never heard from him again… Charming.

2019
Character Building

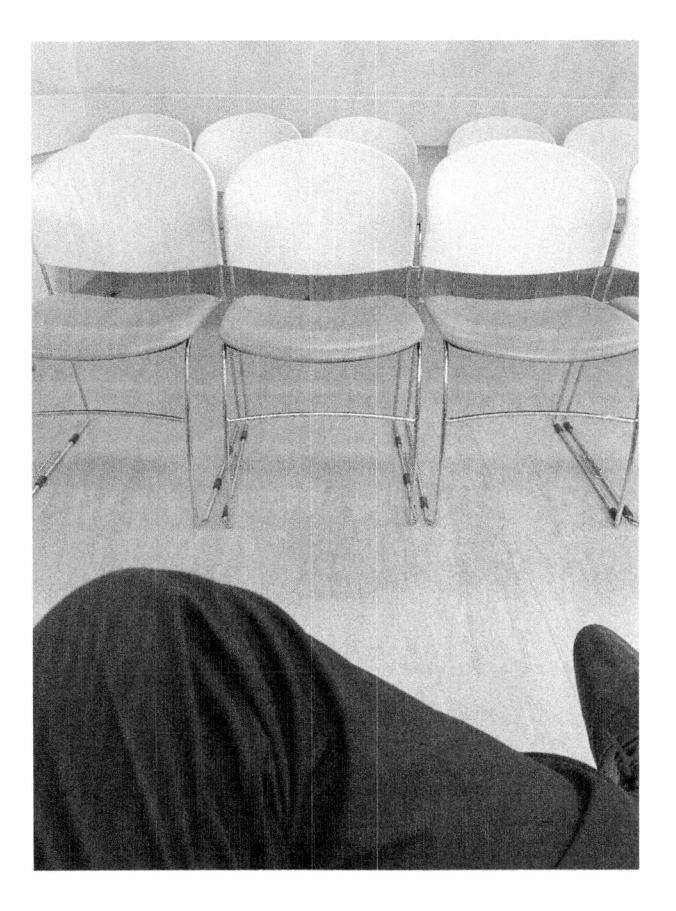

*Note: I haven't forgotten 2020, it just wasn't a funny time, was it…

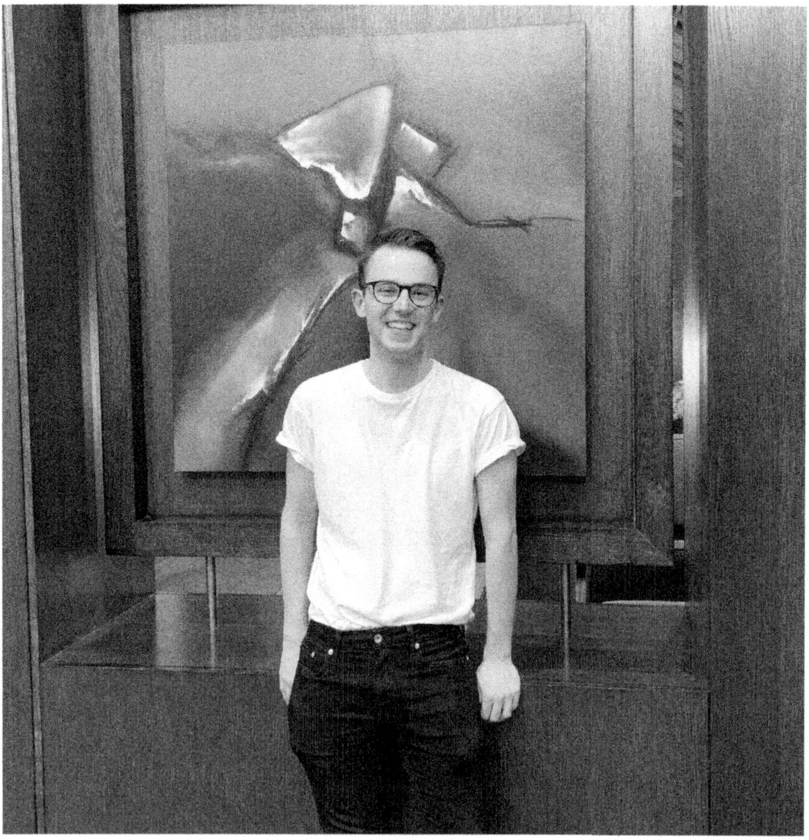

2019

January began with meeting someone who ended up taking advantage of me and single-handedly derailing the next 18 months of life. To cut a long story short, it became my word against his as to what happened between us, and I haven't been able to date carefree ever since.

Whilst having not dealt with what happened, I threw myself back into the dating scene when I was nowhere near ready. Things were lovely with Tesco Guy. We chilled at his house. We watched some films. We baked homemade pizza - *horrid*. We went to the seaside, and it was nice getting to know him. It just didn't sit well with me that he was in the closet. 8 or 9 dates in, nobody knew about me whatsoever. I felt like a dirty secret yet I didn't feel I could tell him that, so I ended up ghosting him. It feels harsh to look back on that now as I clearly left everything unanswered, but his behaviour just told me he wasn't ready. He wasn't ready for a relationship yet and somehow I managed to pick up on that, and I moved on. Not onwards and upwards, but I moved on.

Soon after, I somehow managed to continue working my way through the staff of Tesco and met up with someone else. We went on our date, had a nice chat and I felt pretty optimistic about things. That was until I asked him about concerts. *If you could go and see one person in concert, who would it be?*

He wasn't sure, so I asked three times. *Go on! Who would it be? If you could see anyone, who would it be? Who is the first person that comes to mind?*

pause for thought

"Cliff Richard."

What the fuck? A 25 year old who wants to see Cliff Richard?

Even after a cracker of an answer like that, I remained hopeful a connection would bloom so before I dropped him home, I parked up the car and kissed him. I probably should have asked him to stop, but I didn't have it in me to ask him *not* to mumble compliments between kisses. I don't know how to receive a compliment at the best of times, let alone in my steamed up car in-between kisses. "*You're so handsome*" whispered breathlessly from someone I barely knew just didn't sit right with me.

You're probably reading this thinking this was a one-and-done date, but, for reasons unknown to me now, I actually saw him twice more…

Following our three dates, I made sure it fizzled out after one of my marvellous (*self-professed*) break-up texts. He, however, didn't take the hint, would message me asking to meet up for a drink, and even sent several "*hey man*" messages out of the blue, leaving me no choice but to block him.

Now, I just have to time my trips to Big Tesco well enough to avoid the self-service tills…

Not Knowing Where You Are Going

Life altered at 22.
A Thursday in the early hours,
Strolling around town with my best friend.
Drunken ramblings, aided by fresh air and closed kebab shops.
Stopping outside the college, it hit me.
I'd achieved my life's dream.
"I'm a good teacher."
What do I do now?

Lost

I feel like I'm caught in an orbit in space,
Like a lost satellite,
Spinning round in endless circles,
Progressively getting further from everyone on Earth,
Without any idea of how to bring myself home.
I wonder if anyone is looking up.

Folkestone

I went on a date in Folkestone with a secondary school teacher. We went for pancakes in the chocolate café and had a walk around. There was absolutely no spark of romance whatsoever… The hug goodbye was very limp and I turned away as we said goodbye knowing that I was not going to be speaking to this man ever again.

A few years later, Rachel's Aunt suggests setting me up with someone she knows is single. *"Go for it!"*, feeling excited actually by this potential blind date on the cards. Rachel messaged me saying he was shown a picture of me and he's already dated me… I get sent his picture and it's *him*! At least they tried…

— — —

Another particular guy I was talking to seemed really keen to meet up, yet equally keen for it to *not* be a date.

The penny didn't seem to drop that this would not be what I was looking for, so I went for a walk around the Harbour Arm with him. Another Folkestone date.

He suggested, at several points, going to his flat which I was very reluctant to do. However, much to my annoyance, the light, tolerable rain became heavier and heavier, until the heavens well and truly opened up on us.

Okay, okay, I'll come back to yours.

We kicked our shoes off.
We had some awkward small talk in the living room.
I asked for a cup of tea - *milk and one sugar*.
He went off to make it.
I asked where the toilet was.
He said, "*the door next to the kitchen.*"

If the jockstrap wasn't the giveaway of what he was after from me, the various dildos proudly dotted around the bathroom were…

After finishing my wee, and taking a photo of his toy collection to share with friends later, I was baffled by his lack of soap. I scanned the whole room. No bars. No liquid soaps. Just dildos. In every corner.

I opened the door and called out, "*Where's the soap?*"

He wandered in and proceeded to demonstrate how to use the penis suction-cupped to the wall to dispense some soap. (I'll leave the gesture to your imagination…)

I gave him a judging look. "*Really?*"

He then opened his bathroom cabinet to reveal a rainbow-coloured bar of soap branded '*gay bar*'.

I made my excuses and left soon-after, and I didn't message him again.

— — —

There must be something about my dates in Folkestone because they always end in the friendzone…

I met up with another guy I'd been talking to, who was smothered in tattoos. Not particularly good ones either. The chat flowed though. He was family-orientated, was a social worker and I was keen to get to know him.

In person, he had a very short haircut, one of those where the fringe is cut along a straight line. He had a tongue piercing. He had knuckle tattoos. He was so far from what I was looking for. *What was I thinking?*

There was just no romantic spark whatsoever. We went for lunch in Wetherspoons and I bit the bullet asking how he's finding the date. There was some umming and erring from both of us, before I said *"I think it's just friends"* and I felt a wave of relief come over me. He agreed and we just chatted away then. We said we'd see each other again, which never materialised because I don't actually know what the point would be. We were so different from each other, what would we be doing?!

2021

Love, Again

The Northern One

A whirlwind romance. Although it only lasted two months, the effects of this relationship have taken years to recover from.

As a result of a Tinder's tie-in with Love Island, my profile was opened up nationwide and I liked the look of this slightly rugged, Tom Grennan lookalike. Northern, cute and was as equally frustrated with dating as I was. After a fast-moving talking stage, he arranged to come down to meet me. We planned a few days together, if we liked each other. The spark was there from the moment we met. I liked him, he liked me, and things intensified rapidly. Due to our distance, we agreed to become boyfriends almost immediately. I felt special around him. It was exciting, like the teenage romance I hadn't had. We sat in a bar in Folkestone (*yes, back there…*) and, after playing the piano, he requested U2's *Beautiful Day* and I felt overwhelmed with emotion. I could have cried with happiness. I felt like I'd finally found my person.

With intensity that strong, the highs are high and the lows are low. Although my feelings were developing rapidly, I tried my best to not rush things with him. Meanwhile, he started showering me with cards, gifts and flowers. He quickly revealed his baggage. He had issues with alcohol, making him needy and argumentative. One weekend, he turned up drunk to my house, telling my mum she should be more excited about her birthday as it could be her last. He'd berate me over text for not replying instantly. He'd use all of the swear words under the sun to accuse me of not being interested in him. All whilst I was falling in love with him.

Soon enough, juggling all of these intense emotions led to my health rapidly deteriorating and the negative after-effects of falling in love with him spilled into my working life. Everything started to spiral out of control. My teaching declined, my health declined further and I was dealing with someone accusing me of pulling away. In the end, enough was enough and I called it a day. It took everything within me to do. Breaking up felt like cutting off a working limb, but I felt I had no other choice.

It has taken a long time to move on from him. It has been really difficult to re-adjust to a life without the intense passion and to try not to compare every new connection to that one. If I'm honest, I haven't found a spark remotely close to what I felt towards him and that does make me worry, but I couldn't sustain a connection with someone *that* dependent on me. It's just not worth what it did to me.

Amuse-Bouche

The words hung in the air.
So vulnerably spoken, so carefully crafted.
The silence spoke volumes.
His voice dropped.
The food suddenly became tasteless.
No longer a candlelit dinner bringing us together.
The sticky, wooden table between us,
Seemingly growing larger.
The people next to us feeling livelier,
The more the connection between us dies off.
A full apology is rendered empty.
An awkward goodbye.
A restaurant we don't return to.

Aperitif

Helles Belles

Crisp lager. Bitter. Just like him.

He wouldn't be spotted anywhere without one.

A true alcoholic. A sad past

used to justify his need

to ruin the present.

Suede

Tough material. Some would say "durable".

I'd say "difficult". Hard to manage.

Difficult to maintain. (Dare I say, also like him.)

Also low in %. Common thread? Low in quality.

Oh, and of course there's one from York.

Say no more…

Another Round?

'*The saviour of the broken, the beaten and the damned*'

Pfft. How humble of you.

I've seen you transform the broken, the beaten and the damned.

I wouldn't say they were saved.

I'd argue they all evolved into something worse.

The *broken* became shattered.

The *beaten* became pulverised.

The *damned*…

Let's just label them as the regrettable.

Their *saviour*? More like their enabler.

'The enabler of the shattered, the pulverised and the regrettable'

How's that for *Low Key*?

Recipe for Disaster

Ingredients

- A long distance
- One Northerner with a strange resemblance of Gary Barlow
- A handful of Take That songs
- Too much cask ale
- One bottle of Prosecco too many
- A Sainsbury's bag of shopping ready to be thrown mid-tantrum
- A sprinkle of unwarranted jealousy
- A generous scoop of delusion
- A burden of baggage

Preparation Time - Too Long

1. Begin by establishing you're both on the same page.
2. Turn small talk into meaningful talk.
3. Decide to give this a shot.

4. Arrange a place of meeting - preferably somewhere in the middle, but location is irrelevant.

5. Swoon over the Take That serenades.

6. Prepare to never see Gary Barlow the same way again.

7. Smile when he looks like his photos.

8. Loosen up when you start enjoying yourself.

9. Joke to the random American tourist about your 'teaching him a thing or two' pick-up line.

10. Watch the mood change.

11. Pacify the first few accusations.

12. Then, shout louder.

13. When the Sainsbury's bag gets thrown in the air, phone your best friend within two minutes to explain the situation.

14. Find a well-lit spot to continue the argument.

15. Check into your hotel room.

16. Upon your friend's arrival, leave him wallowing in regret.

17. Talk through your options with your concerned friend.

18. Send your concerned friend home.

19. Choose to endure two more months of this.

Wine: ~~A Love Story~~ A Tragedy

Bright

Fresh

Lively

Powerful

Edgy

Hot

Spicy

Racy

Flamboyant

Smooth

Sweet

Velvety

Blossom

Cliff-edge

Rigid

Grippy

Angular

Spineless

Harsh

Bitter

Aggressive

Complex

Nutty

Musky

Closed

Delicate

Sour

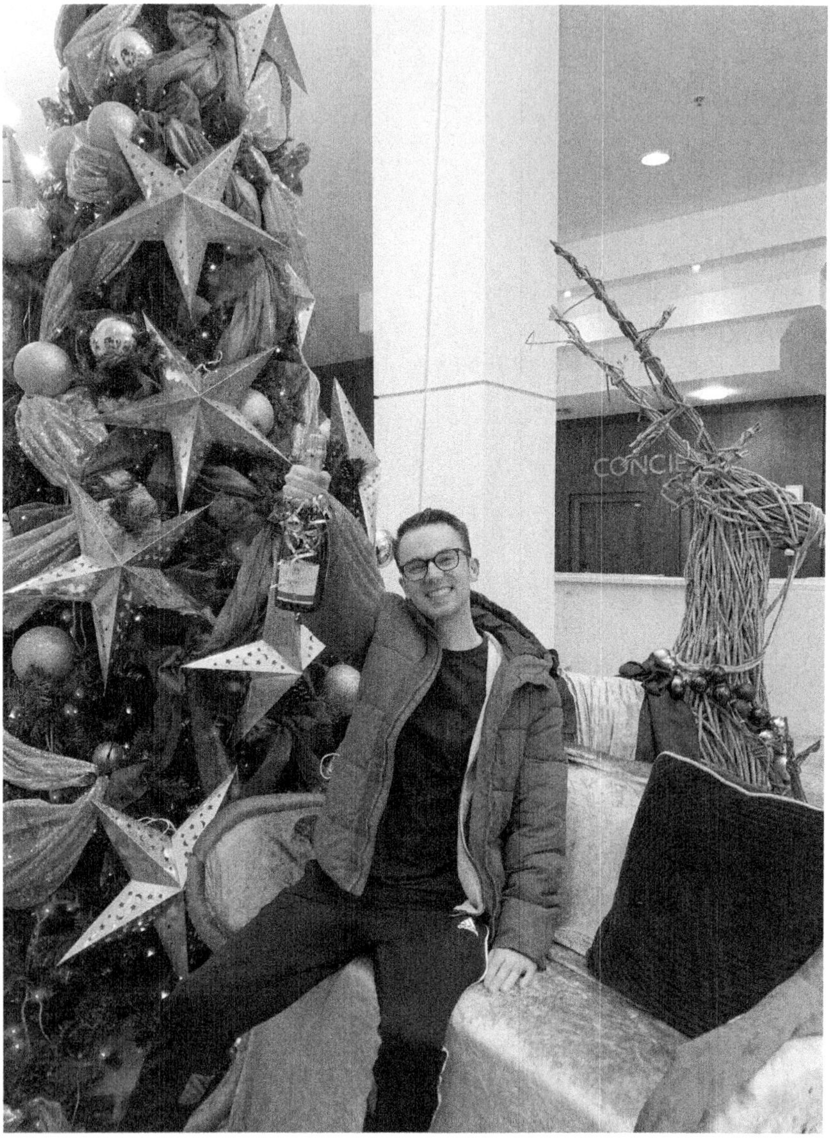

2022

Back on the Horse

The Non-Committal One

Note to self, be careful how much alcohol you drink on dates...

We went for pizza in the place he works and this guy ordered a bottle of Prosecco. I have a pretty low tolerance for alcohol, but there's something about Prosecco that immediately makes me giddy and pairing that with fancying someone was asking for trouble.

I was chatting away, fancying this guy and thinking how well we must be clicking. The pizza was lovely too. The sun was shining. Two girls joined the table and started chatting away, asking how long we have known each other - *just met today* - and they were surprised by how well we got on. I was thinking *I've hit the jackpot here*! At one point, I lurched over the table to kiss him... What possessed me to do such a thing, I don't know.

After eating, we walked around to find the restaurants they had done up on *Interior Design Masters* and I posed for photos outside them. We went in one for a drink, where again the waitress asked how long we've been dating. *Just met today.* "Oh really", she goes, "it's like you two have been together a while". Again, I sat there thinking *this is brilliant*! I must have drunkenly said what a lovely time I was having repeatedly to him.

I remember getting on the train home feeling sad that it was over. Looking back, I reckon he was probably glad to see the back of me...

It fizzled out pretty soon after with no explanation, which hurt me at the time.

He continued to follow me on Instagram and slid into my dms a few times. It was *HIM* who called *ME* out on ghosting *HIM*! Because I hadn't taken him up on his offer of staying over with him in London, apparently I was ghosting him. He apologised when I told him how silly I felt when he'd called me out mid-date on being pushy for a kiss.

I guess a date like that is an example of why communication on the date itself is so important. 'Communication' as in clarifying signals, not as in communicating exactly how you feel all the time unfiltered because you've had one (*four*) too many glasses of Prosecco... We live and learn...

The One Obsessed with Divas

I decided to meet a guy, who had just moved back to Kent, in London for drinks. We went to a bar in Soho and, a couple of drinks in, I was warming to him. It seemed to be going really well. We went off to GAY together and had a great time dancing, and we kissed in the bar too.

After a quiet few days, I got a text saying it wouldn't work as he wants to move back to London. I read it thinking *I wish people wouldn't just waste my time*. Obviously that was just the start of what was to come…

The Date You Couldn't Make Up

I have to say, *this* is the worst date I've been on.

I matched with this particular guy because his Spotify Anthem was S Club's *Bring It All Back*, which caught my eye.

We went for dinner and the red flags just snowballed.

When talking about our jobs, he slagged off his friends, telling me how some worked in shops and how he expected them to be doing more with their lives. I didn't know these friends but I didn't understand why he felt the need to run them down? Aren't you meant to lift your friends up?

Then, he said his dad wasn't comfortable with him being out. I know you can't help your family's reaction to coming out, but his dad would apparently take himself out for lake walks to end himself... The general impression I got was that Dad has a lot of unspoken issues and, if I was brought home to meet him, things would not end well for me.

The next red flag came when I asked him what his choice of karaoke song would be. Madonna's *True Blue*. Niche choice. Didn't see that coming. He then told me about singing it on holiday with a drag queen, proceeding to misgender her repeatedly and ignoring all of my attempts to correct him.

The final straw was when he said he *had* guinea pigs. I picked up on the use of past tense and questioned it, thinking maybe they'd just died a while back. "*My dad found them too aggressive so one day got rid of them...*" This guy had flat-out told me on our first date that his dad had killed his pets. When the waiter came, I did not want dessert, just the bill.

The cheek of it was that it was *HIM* who texted first, saying it was a nice time but we weren't a good match. It was definitely a relief to not have to be the one to broach that, but the audacity for it to be *him* that thought *I* am not *his* match!

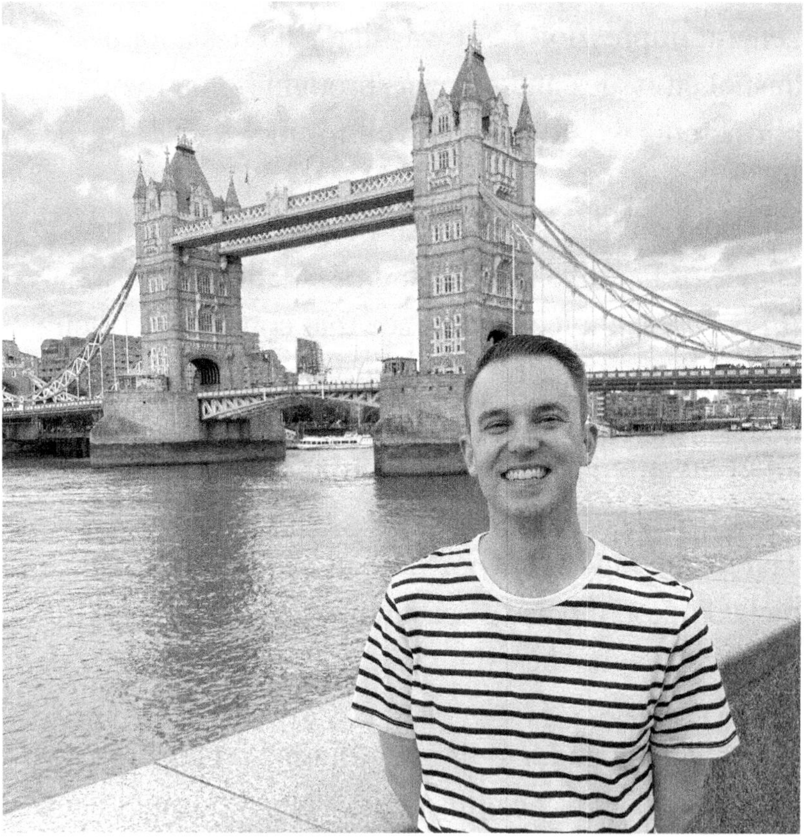

2023

Wasted Time

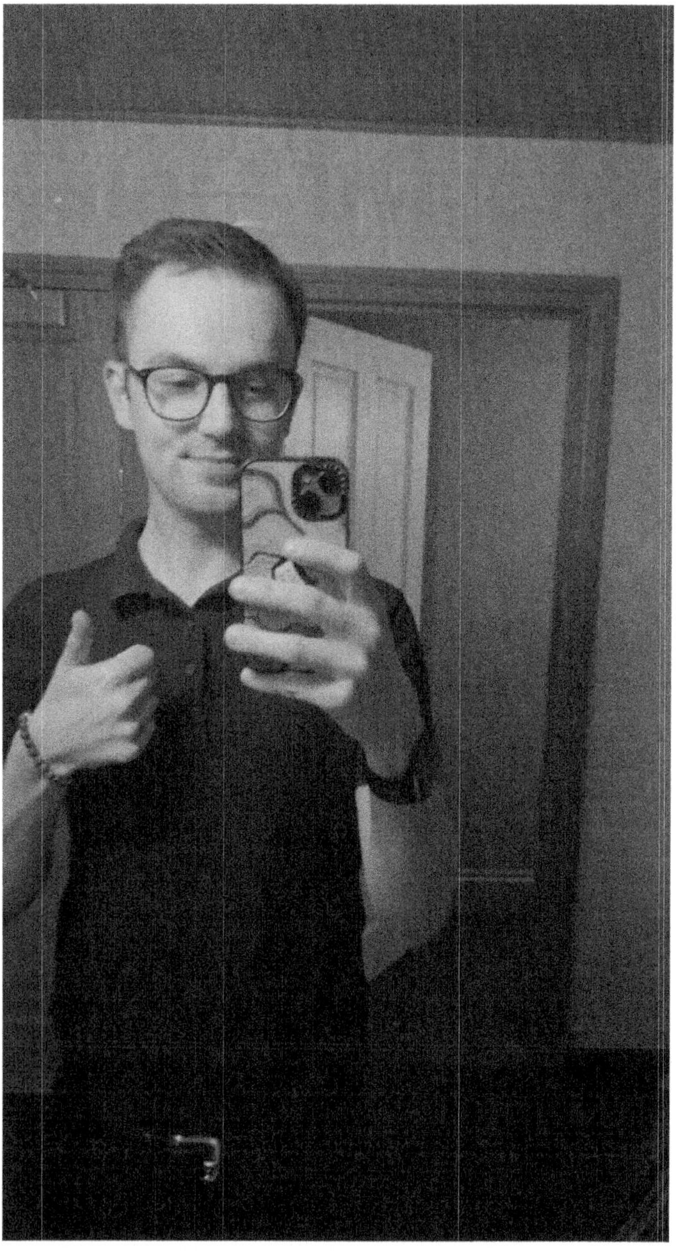

The Socially-Anxious Superhero Fan

March 2023

This guy had everything I wanted. Cute. Creative. Funny. Similar interests. A good hugger. Enjoyed days out. We'd meet twice a week, going for mid-week meals and cute weekend dates. I loved getting to know him and I felt like we were onto something. However, dating him became one step forward and three steps back. He revealed his social anxiety and struggles with opening up to people. Each time I felt ready for a next step, he would freak out. Not ready for exclusivity. Not ready for the boyfriend label. As much as he said it was him and not me, I definitely felt stung by him. Having had enough of his excuses, I asked him to be my boyfriend over dinner out one day and he looked traumatised by my question. I could see in his eyes that this was not going to work. He cancelled several dates with random excuses on the days we were meant to meet, and I developed the mindset of 'fool me once, shame on you, fool me again, shame on me' so I called him out on continually postponing and called it a day.

Over a year later, we matched again on a dating app and, again, he froze up at any mention of dating.

A few months after that, I found out he's in a new relationship, so maybe I was right to take his hesitations personally.

The Time-Waster

May 2023

Generally when anything shitty happens in my love life, I throw myself into something way out of my comfort zone. This time, I applied to my teaching union's LGBT+ conference.

I did my mingling on the social and was pleasantly surprised, considering how awkward and shy I felt, how I persevered and made it through the whole evening. I shared plenty of small talk with people about where they work, what age they teach, what subject, and wondered the whole time what I should be doing with my hands each time my drink had ran out.

Across the room, there was this ginger guy, a bit taller than me, in a nice, white jumper, black jeans and black loafers and I thought he was cute. Soon after, another guy who I thought was fit, who I had just sat opposite at the dinner table and who had managed to drink a beer, a cocktail and two vodkas in the time it took me to have one Aperol Spritz, made his move. 'Drunk, Fit Guy', as he became known to me and my friends, was all over this guy, trying to kiss him. Any chance of me chatting with either guy disappeared so I just focused on dancing with the other strangers, whose names I could barely remember.

I felt pretty confident during the conference itself actually, sharing my opinions and getting to know my table. Back at home, Tinder was suddenly flooded with these new faces from the conference and I happened to match with both men from the night before. Things with 'Drunk, Fit Guy' fizzled out very quickly, but things with the cute guy were much more interesting.

During our small talk, him ignoring me during the entire conference became a running joke. Mostly because it turns out he's one of the people who ran it so it's technically his job to include everyone. We were getting on really well so we arranged a date - a surprise date. This turned out to be indoor crazy golf with a meal and drinks afterwards. We shared two-for-one cocktails and I mustered enough confidence to lean over and kiss him. His response, "Oh, I didn't see that coming!"

Me taking the lead became a running theme.

We had lots of dates. Dinners. Walks around the local lake as the sun was setting. Staying at his house. Meeting his Mum on one of these occasions. Visiting Margate together. He even came for a night out with Rachel too. There were plenty of signs that things were going really well.

When I asked about what stage we were at, things went strange. To me, everything we were doing suggested we could be boyfriends. His response was that it takes a long time for him to get to that point. Crestfallen doesn't do how I felt justice.

To realise just how different you must be feeling to someone else about the same things hurts. He reassured me that he does like spending time with me, but wasn't ready for a label. I chose to stick with it as I believed his reassurance.

Our summer romance carried on and we both headed back to work. We had a dinner date with tapas. We booked a holiday together in Barcelona for the October half term. I also planned to stay at his house for a weekend while his mum was away.

The moment the film we were watching finished, he announced, "I need to take Lily for a walk". Without saying any more, he put his shoes on and led the dog outside. No build-up to going. No asking me if I wanted to go. Not even a goodbye. I was left on the sofa, with nothing on the tv, wondering what was going on. Immediately, I felt like the atmosphere was off. Something must be up.
About 15 minutes later, he came back and didn't really say a lot, sitting on the sofa on the opposite side of the room. Very weird vibe. I think it was me who suggested going up to bed.
We went upstairs, I grabbed my wash bag and I went to get ready in the bathroom.

When I came back, he was laying on the bed watching tv and didn't even look at me. I honestly felt invisible and wasn't sure what was going on.
I started to panic and asked him "is everything okay?". He said "yeah", but didn't even look at me.
I went downstairs, pretending to look for something, to get out of there for a moment and went back up.
I asked if everything was okay again, and he said yes again.
I replied, "because I feel like something's up?".
He said that nothing was up, to which I said "I feel like I like you more than you like me?".
At that point, he said, "I've been meaning to have this chat with you for a while" and then sat up.

He had one of those *'it's not you, it's me'* chats with me. How it takes him a long time to open up because of his baggage. How most people leave and don't wait. It was all a bit *'woe is me'*, yet he could barely even look at me the whole time. For the duration of the conversation, he looked down and couldn't look me in the eyes, whilst I did nothing but stare at him, awaiting some sort of reaction.

He asked me what I was thinking. I said "Well I'm not sure, it's awkward. It's awkward if I stay because of how this has gone. It's awkward if I go because I feel like you're not going to do anything to stop me."

He didn't say much to that, apart from looking sad, and I was getting fed up with all his moping, so I packed up my stuff and left. I hugged him one last time, said bye and drove off.

On the drive home, I was so proud of myself for packing up my stuff and going. I'd felt something was up, I'd spoken up about it and walked away from it. I called Rachel's husband, of all people, to say I was coming home and that was that.

The following day, he texted me and pretty much repeated what he had said in person, so that was like stabbing me a second time. The difference this time was I questioned him about saying he'd been meaning to have the chat with me.
I asked him how long he was thinking about it.
He said about a week.
*Well… t*he previous week was when we had booked our Barcelona trip…
So I then asked him why he let me book it.
His response was that I was so excited about it, which actually felt more hurtful. He knew how excited I was about it yet led me on still. It was actually *him* who used the phrasing "leading you on" to describe his behaviour, which said it all.

We left the chat there. I messaged him saying I'd still like to go on holiday so I begrudgingly paid him back and then paid the extra £125 to change the ticket name to go with Zoe, and said I don't want to go to his birthday brunch now. He did message me a couple of times after to ask about the trip and I said I don't want to talk about that as he'd made that sour for me.

Even now writing this, there is a part of me that still stings from reliving it. In hindsight, I think he knew deep down that he didn't want to be my boyfriend but didn't have the courage to break things off with me. I still see his face in the teaching union's photos and I think, for my own sake, I need to keep away from those events until I feel ready to see him in person again.

I Lost Summer

I thought I'd found what I was looking for.

Late, sunset evenings.
Walking in the park.
Holding hands by the lake.
Kissing until darkness falls.

Sharing songs we like.
Driving to new towns.
Capturing moments in photographs.
Feeling like no one else is around.

Autumn came, things changed.
Realisations we won't be the same.

Summer slipped away.

Another Recipe for Disaster

Ingredients

- One dark evening
- One selfish man
- One badly-trained dog
- An obscure 90s dance song
- A crap TV programme to soundtrack the conversation
- Awkward silence - a generous helping

Preparation Time - This clearly needs several months to prepare, and only half an hour to serve.

Method

1. Enjoy the film together.
2. Relax whilst convincing yourself that everything is normal.
3. Feel grateful for how things are going.
4. Watch him announce that it's time to walk the dog.
5. Wonder why you're not asked to come.

6. Gaze at the TV confused as you hear the door close.

7. Decide what to watch in someone else's home.

8. Try not to look too deeply into *Don't Give Me Your Life*.

9. Await their return.

10. Ask yourself why he chose to sit over there and not next to you.

11. Pretend things are normal as you go upstairs.

12. When your gut instincts begin to pipe up, go and clean your teeth.

13. Stare at yourself in the mirror for a bit.

14. When you enter the bedroom, take notice of how he doesn't look at you.

15. Ask if something is up.

16. When he doesn't answer, take *this* as his answer.

17. Go for a wander downstairs.

18. Use this time to prepare yourself for battle.

19. Re-enter the bedroom and re-ask the question.

20. Without fear, say you feel like you like him more than he likes you.

21. Don't let his lack of eye contact deter you. Use it to fuel your anger - it helps the delivery.

22. Once you feel there's enough moping, pack your things and go.

23. Confidently hug him goodbye - it won't mean anything to you.

24. Under any circumstances, don't look back.

25. Drive home to the soundtrack of Selena Gomez's *Single Soon* - it'll justify the manic grin that'll last the ride home.

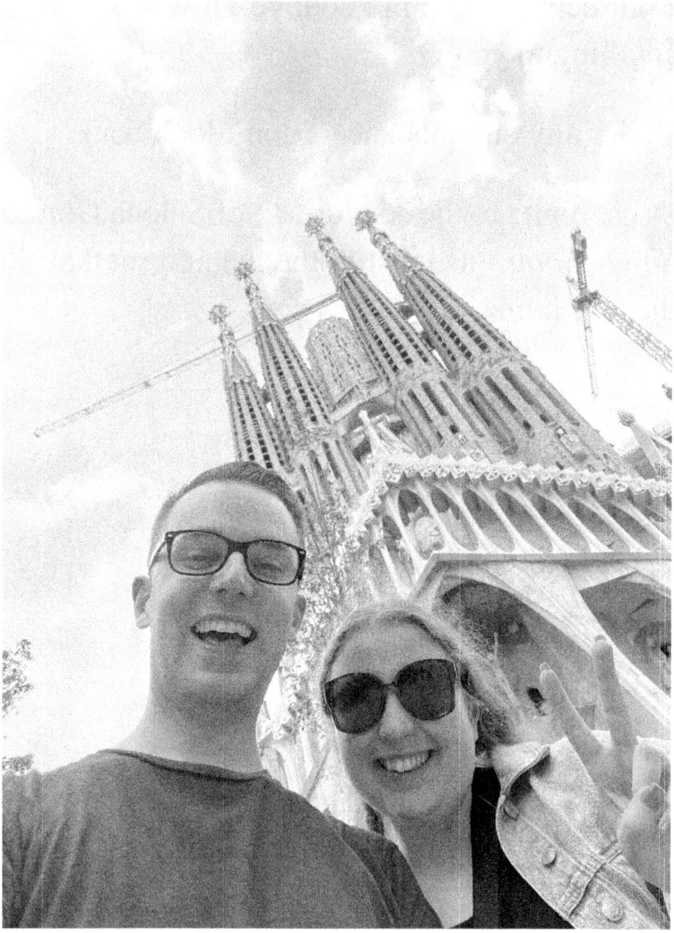

2023

Barcelona and Birthdays

Taking Off

This wasn't how it was supposed to be.

It should have been you; it was your idea.

However, without you, this feels lighter.

Walking through the streets without an itinerary.

Feeling relief for the first time in a while.

My life has paused, you don't matter here.

I try to imagine it's you beside me.

That just doesn't feel the same.

I realise that feels less enjoyable.

Exploring here with you doesn't feel ideal anymore.

Fui a Barcelona…

The First Meal

Our first experience of a restaurant in Barcelona. I opened the menu and straight away was drawn to… spaghetti bolognese. Zoe sat there, laughing, with her bowl of paella, and there I was, my first Spanish meal being spaghetti bolognese (*with an Aperol Spritz, I'd like to add!*). I realised there and then that this would be me doing my holiday my way.

Then, the anxiety started to build. I needed to figure out where the toilets were in there. Here goes nothing… Let's hope my month-long streak on Duolingo pays off… "¿Dónde están los servicios?" I asked tentatively. The waitress smiled, pointing "there" and that was the only Spanish - besides a few "muchas gracias" - that was spoken…

A Sense of Place

Yes! Finally, in our effort of going street to street, there's a bookshop! My aim this holiday was to find a copy of *Heartstopper* in Spanish and there they were, lined up in the children's section upstairs. This place had the hush of a library. The covers were identical to those I've seen dozens of times in Waterstones, the only difference now being the spelling of 'volume' on the spines. I went down the stairs, found the counter and placed the book down, smiling at the cashier.

"¡Hola!" I said. Then she said something that sounded roughly like numbers, which Duolingo clearly hadn't prepared me for. I smiled, nodding, playing along with this facade as if I was fluent in whatever she'd just said, and waved my bank card in the universal way of saying "contactless". She paused. *Uh oh. I've been caught out.* She repeated her phrase. I felt the confusion wash over my face. She said it again, a bit slower… *No idea.* Then, she bluntly goes "bag?", whilst lifting up a plastic bag, and the shame washed over me once more. Who knew a carrier bag would become my Spanish downfall?

Another sense of place

Off-brand Coco Pops together in the glorious, morning sun. Zoe was lost deep in her book, giving me a moment of quiet to just take in what was going on around me.

A street full of multi-storey houses, all identical except the various shops on ground level. Glimpses of other lives through partially-drawn curtains in rooms opposite. A slow rush of cars going up the one-way streets. The occasional horn or motorbike engine in the distance. A low-level murmur of workmen on the scaffolding on the balcony next to ours. Yet another Pitbull song blowing out from inside, where Spanish radio hasn't let go out of the early 2010s. I gaze at my book - my Spanish copy of *Heartstopper* - and this view feels too good to lose myself away from it. You can see identical, beige buildings streets ahead, dusty hillsides in the distance, with a glimpse of the sea if you look over your shoulder. In three days, this will be just a memory. In this morning calm, it's the first time in weeks where I can just sit silently and listen.

An Apology?!

Travel writing has taken me back to standing by the yellow line on Stratford International's platform, receiving an essay of a text from an unknown number.

A long-awaited apology that I realised I didn't need to have achieved closure.

In feeling over it, it just made me wonder what he wanted out of reaching out.

What was he trying to achieve from (*finally*) apologising?

He said he'd treated me badly.

He said he'd treated *a few people* badly.

Why?

Why is he working on that now?

Why does he feel the need to apologise to me?

28 (Ryan's Version)

My birthday.

Previously defined by chaotic gatherings

of mismatched people.

Tonight, a happy one.

Gold, sparkly t-shirt.

Personalised birthday cake

Made with love.

Curated, carefully-crafted soundtrack.

Hilarious, humming board game.

Friendships finally like-minded.

A gathering finally without judgement.

A peaceful journey to the club.

Sing-along staples fuelling the lively atmosphere.

Undeterred by the smoke machine.

A sober success.

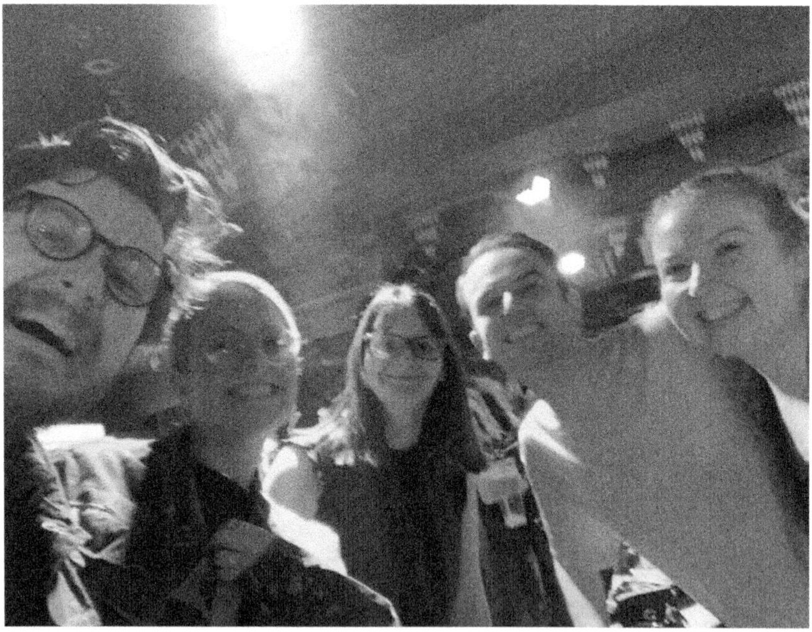

2023 - 2024

Trying to Move On

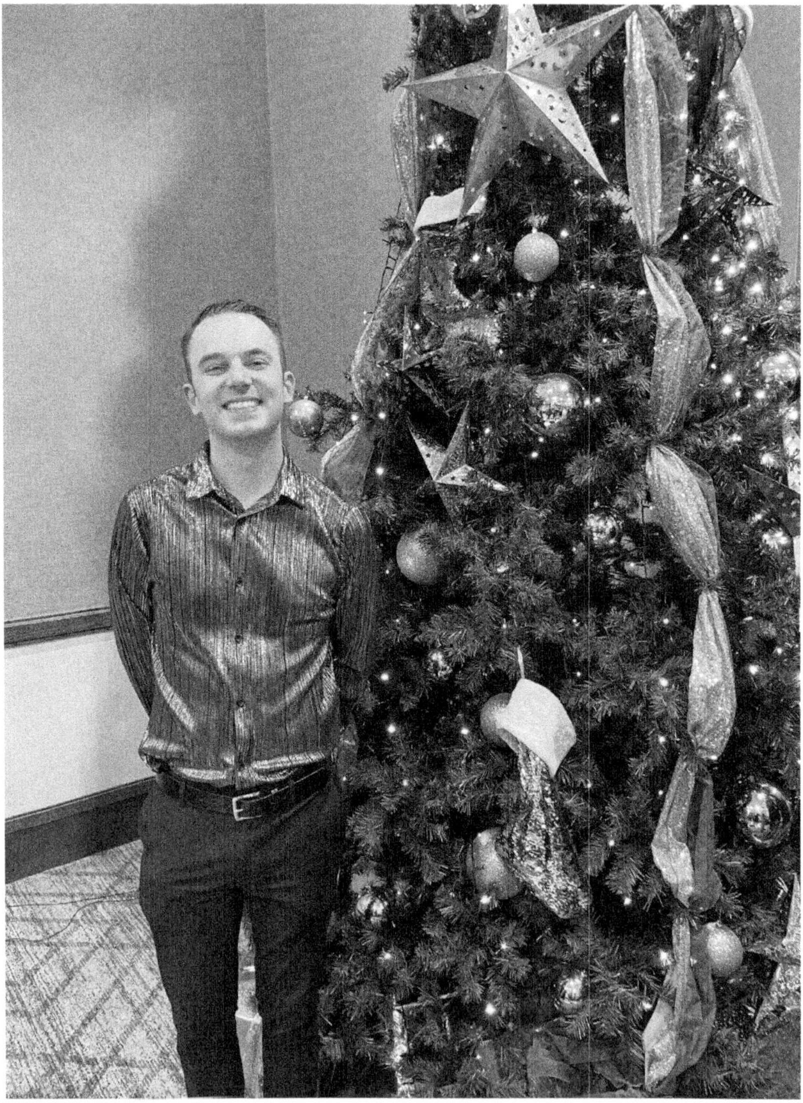

The One I Re-Connected With

Sometimes what ifs make you realise you've wasted a fair few years wondering what could have been…

I was talking to this guy who turned out to be from the year below me in school. The fairytale romantic in me was thinking of how much we'd have in common and how much our paths must have crossed, yet I had absolutely no recollection of this man whatsoever. Back then, I was scheduling dates with him but he kept cancelling, saying he wasn't ready to date yet and was still in the closet.

Several years later, after my summer of failed romance, he reappeared on a dating app. We matched and the what ifs resurfaced. He claimed to be in a good place now, lived near me and has his own place. He is out now to his family and was ready to find his person. We arranged to go for a walk around the local lake and the park.

On the day, the first thing I noticed was how hooked his nose was. We hugged, pretty awkwardly to be honest, and started chatting away. However, I couldn't help but notice each time I turned to the side to talk to him just how hooked that nose was. His photos clearly had captured his *good* side. It dawned on me that the reason why his photos had never changed from before must have been that the selection had been *that* carefully chosen…

Over a disgusting gingerbread latte, I had no issues with saying it was nice date but there was no romantic spark, and he agreed. It's pretty telling isn't it when you hug to say goodbye and just smile and walk away, without even a thought of *'should I kiss them?'*.

The Northern-Irish One

This guy was from Northern Ireland. I really fancied him and the chat was good. We went for dinner and then bowling, and we kissed goodbye outside the bowling alley. We saw a fireworks display together and I noticed it was me going in for the kiss. He invited me into his at the end and that felt like things were going well. At the end of our third date, I asked if he wanted to see me again, like I always did, after I'd just offered him a lift. "*Errr… maybe as friends. It's not you, I think I need more time to get over my ex. I don't think I'm ready for a relationship yet.*" I took it quite well, I think, saying *"that's okay"*, but deep down thinking '*oh shit… I now have to drive him home…*'. I put Taylor Swift's *1989* on, which made the drive so much longer… I parked outside his house, with *Style* blasting out at us and it felt like he wouldn't get out. He was talking about having a nice time, clearly trying to soften the blow, but I was thinking '*please just get out*'. He hugged me, got out and I put on Maisie Peters' *John Hughes Movie* for the drive home, in an attempt to get some of the embarrassment of being rejected out of my system.

I know deep down that it wouldn't have worked out with him. We're probably a bit too similar. What really helped me get over him was how he turned up to our most recent catch-up (*as friends*) with a moustache. Sometimes they just don't suit people…

The Disney Fan

I bonded with the next guy over a shared love of Pixar characters. It was cute. We saw a band together. We kissed in a car park whilst snow fell in the middle of December. We sat in the train station together waiting for his train to come. We ventured off to London together to an exhibition. We basically lived out another teenage dating experience.

This was, however, another case of life getting in the way. I was struggling mentally, with juggling my personal and working life and I was fighting a lot of self-doubt with who Mr Young was. This definitely spilled into my feelings towards him. As much as I enjoyed being around him, I second-guessed everything. Not just questioning how the dates actually went, but questioning if I was even actually attracted to him.

After five dates, I was poorly from trying to juggle everything and I felt the need to call it a day. I just needed to rein everything in and spend some time focusing on myself. I'd love to say he understood…

but he really didn't. He soon revealed his true colours, becoming one of those people who post cryptic quotes online and then frantically deny it's about you when you confront them about it. Definitely better off without *that* energy in my life.

The Year of First Dates

2024. Under the veil of trying to work out what I'm actually looking for, I found myself on a series of first dates. I had hoped for follow-ups, *to some, not all*, but they just didn't work out. Life just got in the way again. Some were ill. Some were just too busy. Some lost my interest. Some didn't reply. Overall, I just didn't feel the spark with any of them, although I've definitely come away from these dates with a greater sense of what I do and don't want in a partner. I also didn't change myself to make any of the matches work out, which definitely feels like growth to me.

Summit

I tug open my crisp packet, feeling a sense of accomplishment.

We made it to the top.

Arthur's Seat. What I came to Edinburgh for.

And then comes the rain…

I suppose when you're this high up, it comes with the acceptance that you will just be wet now.

A theme that lasted all three days in Scotland.

The descent was more difficult than the climb.

Not because of the steepness, but due to the fear of sliding over.

All of this made the relief to be sat down in the dry with a pot of a tea and a bag of fudge more satisfying.

Stag

My aunt mentioned your name. She said you sounded quite nice.
I smiled back, saying you're old news, wondering how much she knew.

If only she'd seen your behaviour on my birthdays when the focus was on me and not you.
If only she saw me when I saw the dating app still on your phone one year in.
If only she'd heard you use the phrase "window-shopping" to justify having it still.
If only she knew you'd always say it's not like we'll be together forever.

— — —

There were several moments during the wedding that felt like a torch was being passed between us.
I think that stems from when you first told me you'd met her whilst I told you I'd left him.
I felt so joyful to see the pair of you in love, saying your vows and sharing your speeches.
Then it hit me... it'll be my turn next.

Something Light…

"I had an affair."

I abruptly stifled my laughter.

She wasn't laughing. She was serious.

Suddenly, our light lunchtime catch-up

Turned into something much more vulnerable.

Much more uncomfortable.

The light around us juxtaposed the darkness

Spilling out of her as I asked her

To talk about it.

Toasted sandwiches became picked at.

Crumbs wiped away nervously.

Ceramic mugs held tentatively.

The awkward silences awaiting judgement

From both sides of the table.

The perfect illusion shattering.

The fairytale gaining an unexpected twist.

Across from me, you've never looked lonelier,

Why didn't you just tell me?

Cameo

Thumps of drum and bass become muffled.

There's a frost in the air tonight.

Rowdy people huddle under luminous, red heaters.

Cigarettes are passed between drunken friends.

Cackles carry sweet scents of Elf Bars.

Questionable characters pass packets of powders unnoticed.

A man, perching on a wooden table, snorts a powder, undeterred by the ramble.

Girls' drunken laughter grows louder and louder.

Discussion of A-Level results begins around the table.

"You're 28?! You only look about 20!"

That was the moment that I felt like nightlife wasn't for me anymore.

Hugging my friend goodbye, we headed separate ways.

Hers a date's car, mine the taxi heading home.

Content, alone, with my bed to myself.

Growth.

2024

Destroying Mr Young

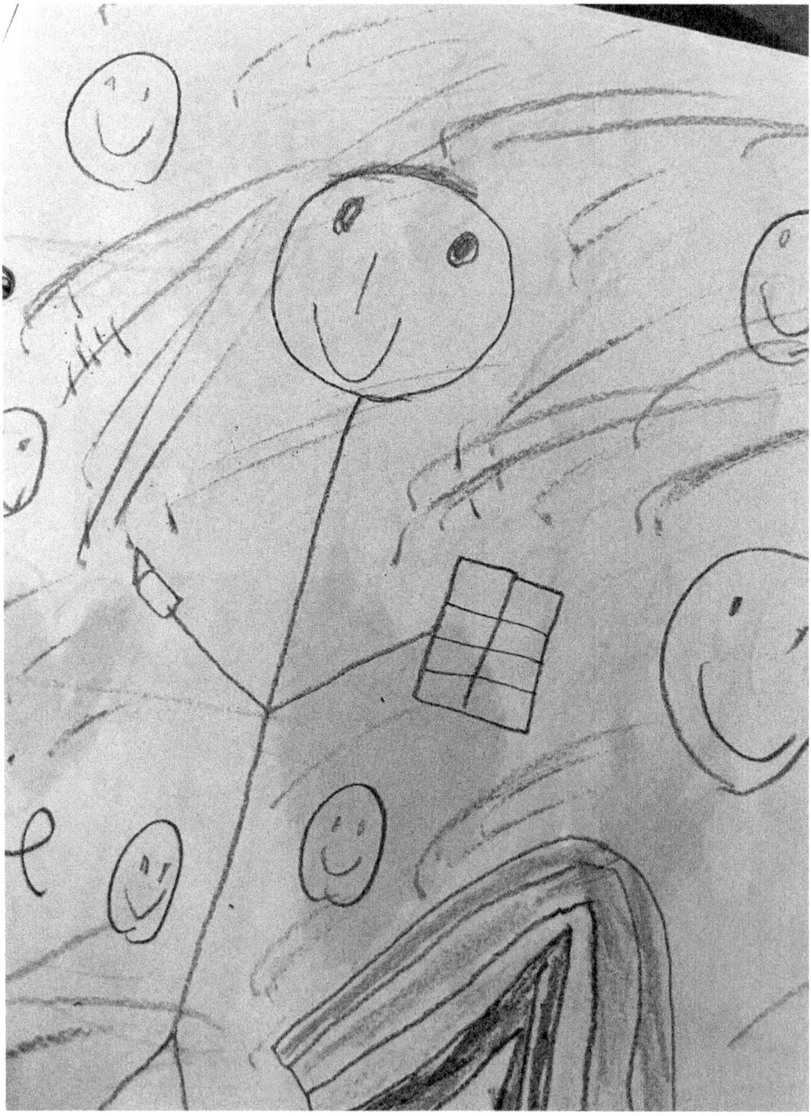

Looking Out

I've only been here for two years.
I'm designed to be a happy place.
I'm meant to be a safe space.
I'm the centrepiece for a growing community.
They come from far and wide to be a part of me.
My gates open at the same time, day in, day out.
The same children run through, rushing to be first in.
Worried pupils question what's changed since yesterday.
Nervous infants delay leaving their parents behind.
A refuser gets dragged by the hand through the office doors.
I, however, am excited for the day ahead.
There's an endless list of possibilities in my classrooms.
I wonder what learning these teachers have planned.
Every day, these adults park up, one by one,
Each one with something special to offer.
The one in the light blue car sticks out to me.
He has been one of the longest serving here.
He parks in the same space each day,
Always pausing for a few seconds too long,
Placing his bag over one shoulder,
Checking each car door handle in sequence.
I have watched him change over these two years.
He is no longer reminiscent of the man who first arrived.

He doesn't seem as care-free anymore,
Yet he appears to be more reflective.
Despite this, there's a warmth wherever he goes,
Although I don't think he can see that.
When he's here, the atmosphere becomes a warm hug.
When he isn't, the children unsettle,
Seeking the comfort he offers them.
Today, they're in luck.
He's greeting each and every one of them.
I know today's going to be a good day.

Where I Was

I'm in my school's corridor.
A walkway I've walked down many times now.
The same old plastic display cabinets.
    I've avoided updating those for way too long.
The empty, wooden Kallax units.
    They were meant to be filled and decorated.
    What was once my display had been thrown
    around a while back.
This corridor feels very dull for a school.
There's an absence of colour and vibrance.
If it wasn't for a pupil's scream echoing from the hall,
You might have mistaken this for a derelict building.
This walk feels longer than it usually is.
It bothers me that this doesn't feel like a happy place.
It feels like something's missing here,
But I haven't figured out if that's a gap I can fill.

Grievance

Two months ago…

The joy was gone.
Enough was enough.
Everything became pointless.
Little things became an effort.
The rollercoaster of life continued.
The highs were getting higher,
The lows were getting lower.
Was it the abundance of anxiety,
Or the absence of everything?
Everyone around me watching me slip away.
A sudden talk of options,
Knowing deep down there's only one route.
It was time to take this seriously.
Talking alone wasn't enough anymore.
A week away in my own world.
Made the world out there less scary.

"Are you feeling any better?" people ask.
I'd just smile, because, *honestly?*,
I don't even know.
I wasn't expecting a lightbulb to just flick on,
That everything's okay now,
But things just don't feel much different.
28, and it feels like I'm figuring out how my brain works for the first time.
I don't react how I used to.

I don't feel anything anymore,
Yet somehow I feel everything.

I kept thinking I'd hit rock bottom,
I'd bounce back and then hit a lower state.
My most recent rock bottom was a phone call to my best friend.
I couldn't open my eyes.
I laid on my bed,
Mumbling away about my day,
Seeing no point in living anymore,
Saying things without caring what reply I got,
Burdening her with my mindset.

My headteacher believes my teaching is full of weaknesses.
My executive headteacher feels *that* judgement of my teaching is fair.
They don't seem to see what this is doing to me.

For too long, I've been drowning.
Giving this group of children everything,
Until I had nothing left to give myself.
I *almost* broke.
I emphasise almost here.
I walked away for a week.
Then returned.
Became Mr Young again.
Doing what I do best.
Getting no better thought of.

I have reached a point where believing in myself has become dysphoric.
I have these people, who are seen to be important, not believing in me.
It's become warped to believe in myself now.

Is my five year plan a point of ridicule?
Is my view of myself really distorted?

It's really hard to keep waking up every day,
When you're the only person believing in yourself.
I stand at the front of this class,
Seeing 20 safe, smiling children,
Who have all flourished since I first met them last year.
But people are trying to provide me with evidence to disprove that.
People that don't know these children.
People that don't know me.

One thing I do know is that I'm tired.
I'm tired of thinking so much.
I'm tired of worrying so much.
I'm tired of trying to prove myself.
I'm tired of believing that I have to be better.
I'm tired of not feeling good enough.

I have waited days, weeks, months, years,
Maybe even decades for someone else,
To put a hand on my shoulder,
And tell me I am good enough.

Maybe I need to let go of that hope.
Maybe that'll never happen.
Maybe that's a feeling that has to come from within.

Unrequited Love

I'm in an abusive relationship with my job.

My job tells me I'm not good enough.
My job gives me sleepless nights.
My job asks for more than I can give.
My job makes me question what I deserve.
My job leaves me bruised inside and out.
My job gives me anxiety most days.
My job has driven me to medicate.
My job requires coping strategies now.
My job forces me to become someone else.
My job has taken away my identity.

I loved my job once.
It was what I'd always dreamed of.
The classroom welcomed me with open arms,
Its hug growing tighter until it wouldn't let me go.
I once thrived in its vibrant energy.

My proud smile is now just a grimace,
A brave mask worn to deceive,
Convincing 24 others that everything is okay.
Behind the mask, I'm screaming for help,
Yet no one can see.

The Mirror Has Always Been There

When I've had to tell myself I'm doing a good job.

When I've scratched away at the hen party make up.

When I've had to convince myself that I'm better than the other candidates.

When I've had to convince myself that they're not right and to follow my gut instincts.

When I've counted my breaths in attempts to calm myself.

When I've thought through the steps of how to leave him.

When I noticed the white lines across my back.

When I started to notice how my body isn't like theirs.

When I tried to filter out the comments about my weight.

When I've hated what I've seen.

Not Perfect, Like Me

For as long as I can remember, I have pushed for perfection.
This pursuit has always left me feeling not good enough.
There's a newly-found power in admitting to not being perfect,
Like a weight being lifted from my shoulders.
It's been a long time coming.

Grounding Myself

The new classroom.

A place I've stepped into.

Prepared by someone else.

Prepared for someone else.

A cocoon for me to blossom out of.

Welcoming in 23 nervous, tentative pupils.

Dismissing 23 relieved ones.

A six-hour journey of scratching the surface.

The re-establishment of Mr Young.

A sign of joy to come when closing the door.

Looking at empty tables and stacks of chairs.

Exhaling, not with relief, but from calm.

"Maybe it's a feeling you need to return to?"

It feels so good to be moving on.
The reinvigoration from re-establishing myself,
Embracing somewhere new.
Notifications are sitting unread.
Relationships calling me back.
Reminders of what I'm leaving behind.
For the first time, I realise I wield
The power to leave it behind.
I've spent the summer clinging on
To what I'd built back there.
The shreds that they tore apart.
Thinking that's what I'll rebuild myself from.
Now I realise *that* ending doesn't matter.
What happened bears no meaning here.
I thought I needed to go back to move on,
But, with distance, that necessity is gone.

"Laidback"

I haven't always been this way.

I curated a new version of myself,

An effort to escape my past.

The previous version of me was so badly hurt,

That I believed it would be much easier to create a new one.

Putting my pieces back together

Has taken more energy than I ever thought,

And I realise no one knows why I am the way I am.

I made the choice to put down the mask,

And explain myself without fear of judgement.

Now people understand,

That I haven't always been this way.

2024

Regrouping.

Planning.

"What can we do to help you?"

They don't say "you don't know how good you are" anymore.

I'm doing my best. Why can't they see that?

Finally in control.

How quickly things change.

This is all too much.

Signed off.

"We miss you."

Here goes nothing.

Back on the hamster wheel.

Drop-ins.

"There are some definite weaknesses."

What can I do?

I want someone who believes in me.

Grievance.

"She has plenty of experience."

"I can see a real difference."

"I didn't see any teaching."

Mixed messages.

"It's not personal."

"They won't get this year back."

Realisation.

Enough is enough.

Taking control.

Resignation.

"Why didn't you fight it?"

Tears, not mine.

Leaving with my head held high.

Beginning recovery.

To those I've lost,

It has taken me a long time to let you all go. A lifetime of work to no longer see myself as the problem. It has been a journey that I'm still treading carefully on. I tell myself that you all came into my life and left again for good reasons. (Mostly in the hope that, one day, I'll believe it wholeheartedly.)

I must acknowledge that I have changed over the years. Just like you outgrow clothes, haircuts and music tastes, I have outgrown these previous versions of myself. With that in mind, it is understandable that friendships, that would have worked then, won't work now. That's okay.

I didn't understand that things change back then. Maybe that's why growing apart hurt so much.

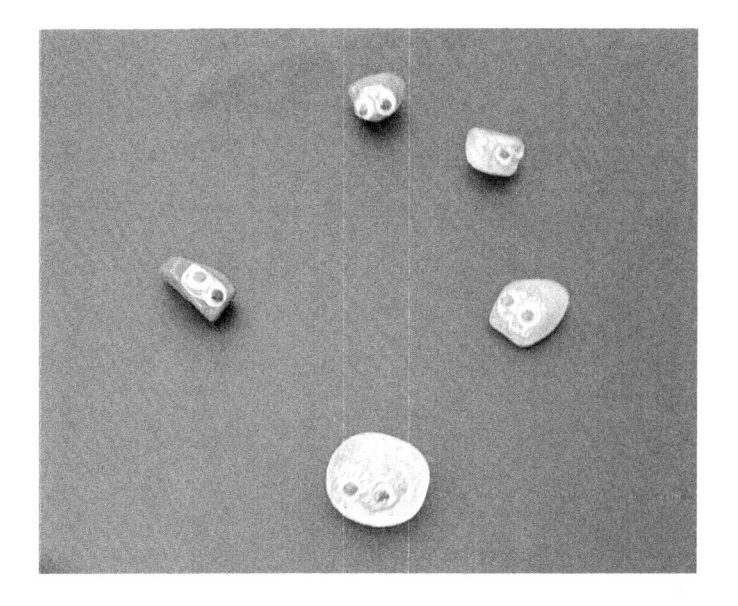

Acknowledgements

Firstly, I would like to thank both Rachel and Zoe, my best friends. These two have been by my side through everything that I have written about and have helped me get to the other side of it all.

Zoe, how much we've both grown over the past decade! Can you imagine going back in time and sharing all the things we have been through with our younger selves?! Thank you for always being ready with the advice that I have definitely needed to hear and I apologise for usually choosing to do the opposite… Maybe one day I'll listen…

Rachel, I am grateful for your ability to pick me up whenever I am down. For seven years and counting, you have supported me through my ups and downs and become my biggest supporter. Words will never be enough, but thank you for being there!

I would also like to thank Sita and the writers from her writing workshops for creating a friendly and supportive space that has allowed me to scribble my thoughts, feelings and experiences into my notebook and share glimpses into my world. Around the *Words and Wine* table, sharing *Grievance* was the first time that I opened up about how my year was going with strangers, and I'm grateful for Nicki for suggesting that I should send my writing out into the world. The seed was definitely planted that evening!

Finally, I should probably thank the subjects of my writing. Although I may not be thankful for what some of you have done to me over the years, I am very thankful for the person that you have all made me become.

Printed in Great Britain
by Amazon